OREGON COAST AQUARIUM°

For Bruce McKean

A Place of Wonder

The Oregon Coast Aquarium is a private non-profit, educational facility. The goal of the aquarium is to educate a broad spectrum of the public about the unique and abundant natural resources of the Oregon coast so that they can be responsible stewards of those resources now and in the future.

All educational material in "The Seven Seas of Billy's Bathtub" has been gathered and verified in cooperation with Allen Monroe and his staff at The Oregon Coast Aquarium.

Library of Congress Catalog Card Number: 95-078728

ISBN: 1-885223-27-7

Produced in the United States of America by SunWest Graphics, Inc., Bridgetown Printing, and Lincoln & Allen Bindery

Printed on recycled paper using soy-based inks

Distributed to the book trade by Publishers Group West

Beyond Words Publishing, inc.

4443 NE Airport Road

Hillsboro, Oregon 97124-6074

503-693-8700

1-800-284-9673

Oregon Coast Aquarium

2820 SE Ferry Slip Road

Newport, Oregon 97365

503-867-3474

Introduction

Over half of the world's surface is covered by water. In these oceans and seas live millions of fish, birds, and animals. Human beings have to share the planet with all of these creatures, so, at times, things can get a little crowded.

How can we make sure that our oceans will remain protected from dangers like pollution?

If we're to live in harmony with these creatures, it's very important that we learn as much as we can about our ocean's wildlife and their world. Education will allow us to best protect and conserve delicate habitats and food sources. By reading books, taking classes, and visiting zoos and aquariums, we will become a society prepared to make sure that some of Earth's most amazing treasures will be around for future generations to enjoy!

Sydney Butler

Executive Director

American Zoo and Aquarium Association

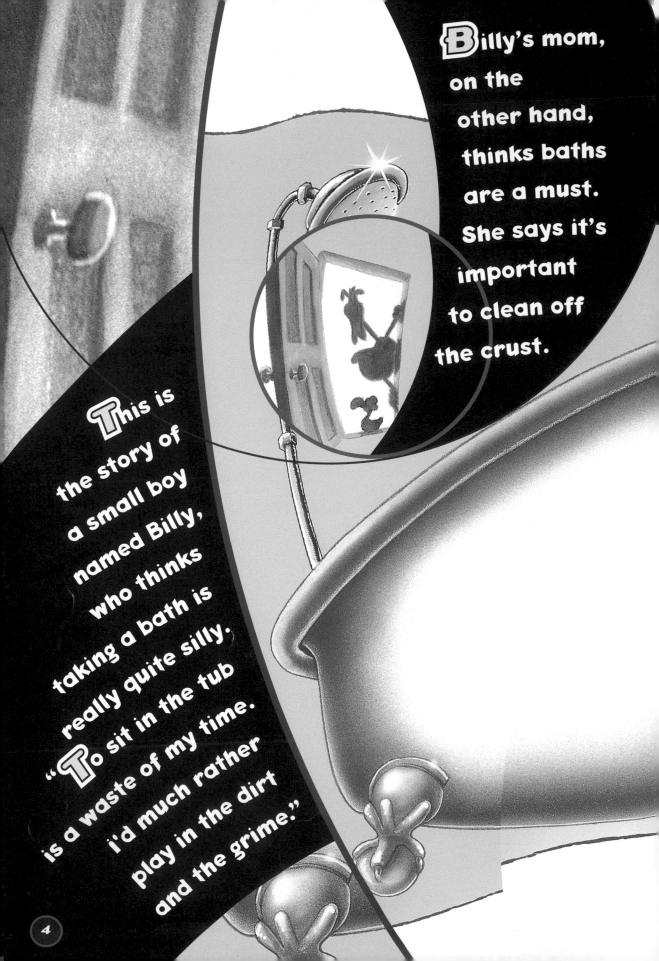

Billy's mom, on the other hand, thinks baths are a must. She says it's important to clean off the crust.

This is the story of a small boy named Billy, who thinks taking a bath is really quite silly. "To sit in the tub is a waste of my time. I'd much rather play in the dirt and the grime."

Soooo...every night Billy
and Molly crawl in the tub,
for a fate worse than death:
a good soapy scrub.

5

"No matter
how hard i try,
i get soap in my eye,

and my fingers and toes turn to prunes.
i don't like taking baths—they make me upset.
it's really quite simple: i hate getting wet!"

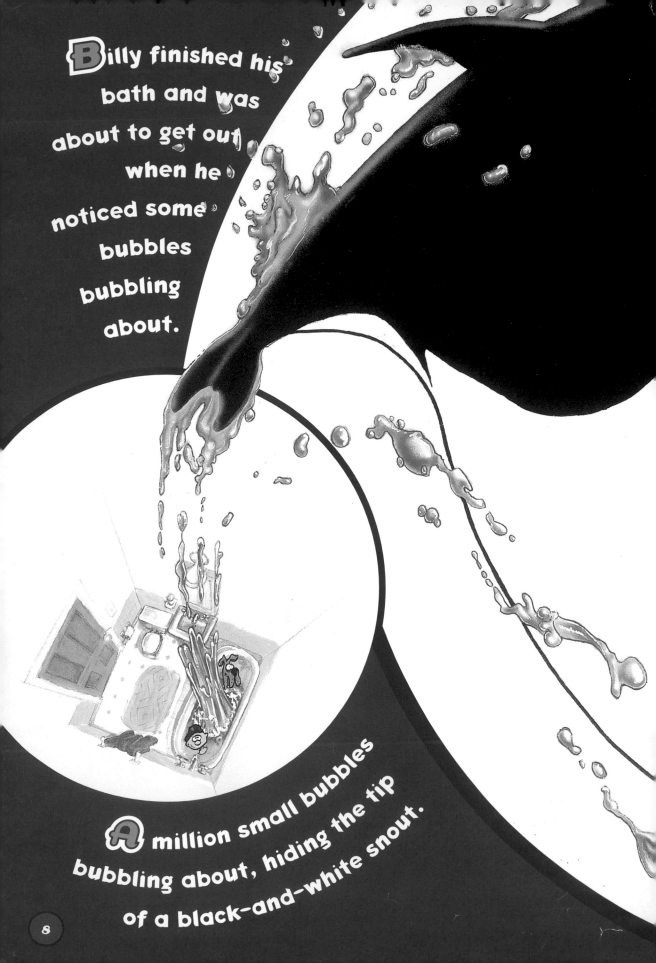

Billy finished his bath and was about to get out when he noticed some bubbles bubbling about.

A million small bubbles bubbling about, hiding the tip of a black-and-white snout.

8

Billy's body went limp and his dog turned quite pale, because out of the tub burst a huge orca whale!

9

"I was just swimming by," sang the whale,
"when i heard what you said,
and i cannot believe that it's bathtime you dread.

"So wipe the frown off your face and quit singing the blues; it's time we all went on a magical cruise."

The anchor was lifted, the bathtub broke free,
and with a mighty "Heave ho!"
they sailed out to sea.

Operculum
(bony covering for gills)

Dorsal fin

Tail fin

Anal fin

Pectoral fin

Fish are covered with a layer of slimy mucus that helps them to slip through the water and protects them against parasites.

Black-and-Yellow Rockfish

How do fish breathe under water?

Fish need oxygen just like humans do. Humans get oxygen from the air, but fish must get "dissolved" oxygen from the water. Fish pump water over their gills, and oxygen passes through the thin gill membranes directly into the fish's blood.

"You see," said the whale, "fish take baths all the time. They're always quite clean..."

Big fish, small fish

The world's biggest fish is the whale shark. It can grow to 50 feet in length and weigh 20 tons. The smallest fish is the Filipino Dwarf Goby, which is less than half an inch long.

French Angelfish

Short Bigeye

14

Blue Tang

Longspine Squirrelfish

Queen Triggerfish

Spotfin Butterflyfish

"No dirt, dust, or grime."

A **fish** is a creature that is usually covered with scales, breathes with gills, and lives under water. All fish are vertebrates, meaning that they have a backbone and a skeleton.

Up, up, and away

Flying fish have large fins that act as wings. These fins allow the fish to glide along the surface of the water at speeds up to 30 miles per hour.

Flying Fish

"**A**ll these creatures are happy, to the very last trout, so i can't understand what you're moaning about."

Hide and seek

The flounder has mastered the art of camouflage. It can become almost invisible by changing colors and patterns to match the ocean floor.

Eye, eye, captain

When flatfish are born, they look like other fish, but within weeks they change. Their bodies become thin and flat and one of their eyes shifts to the other side of their head until both eyes are on the same side.

Loggerhead

Flounder

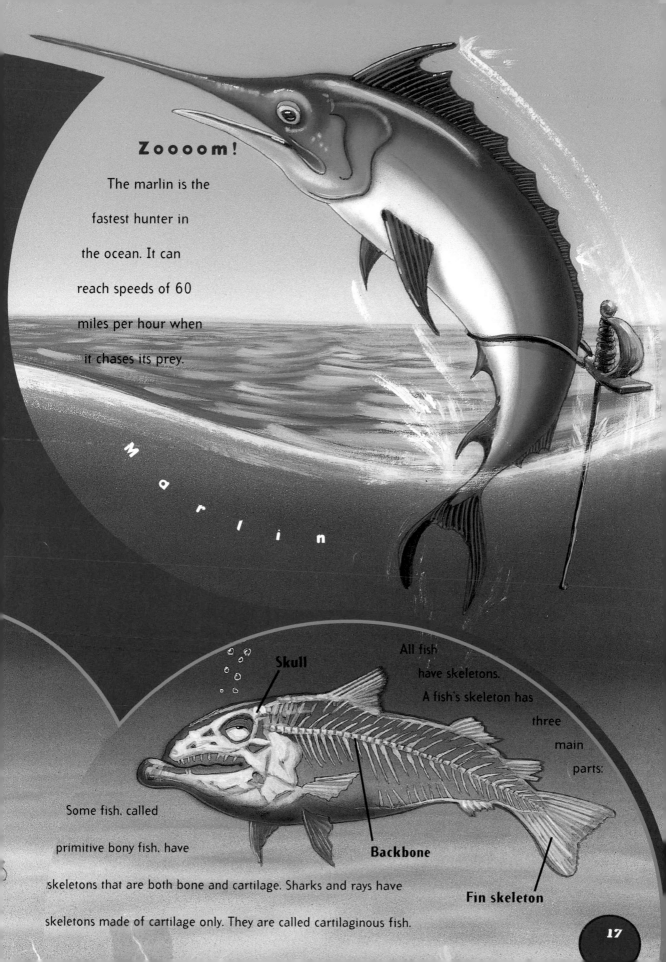

Zoooom!

The marlin is the fastest hunter in the ocean. It can reach speeds of 60 miles per hour when it chases its prey.

Marlin

All fish have skeletons. A fish's skeleton has three main parts:

Skull

Backbone

Fin skeleton

Some fish, called primitive bony fish, have skeletons that are both bone and cartilage. Sharks and rays have skeletons made of cartilage only. They are called cartilaginous fish.

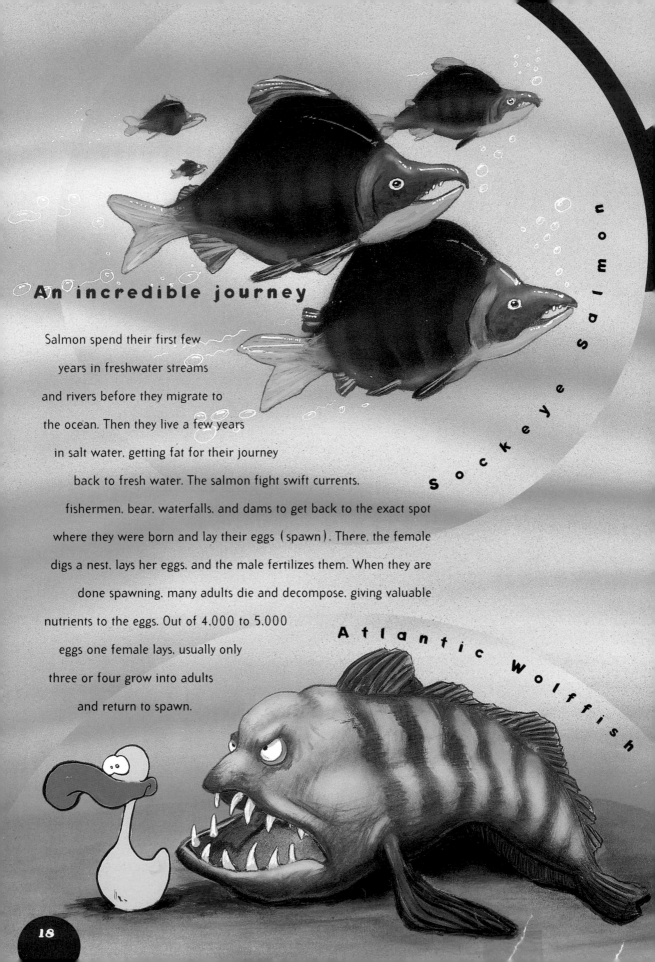

An incredible journey

Salmon spend their first few
years in freshwater streams
and rivers before they migrate to
the ocean. Then they live a few years
in salt water, getting fat for their journey
back to fresh water. The salmon fight swift currents,
fishermen, bear, waterfalls, and dams to get back to the exact spot
where they were born and lay their eggs (spawn). There, the female
digs a nest, lays her eggs, and the male fertilizes them. When they are
done spawning, many adults die and decompose, giving valuable
nutrients to the eggs. Out of 4,000 to 5,000
eggs one female lays, usually only
three or four grow into adults
and return to spawn.

Sockeye salmon

Atlantic Wolffish

Billy cried, "You big goofy fish, are you completely insane? i think all of this water has gone straight to your brain!"

Lionfish

The top five "weird but real" fish names

Jolthead Porgy

Greater Soapfish

Onespot Fringehead

Shortspine Thornyhead

Monkeyface Prickleback

if looks could kill

The beautiful lionfish is one of the most poisonous fish in the sea. It has glands at the ends of its fins which contain a powerful venom. The venom can cripple predators and be deadly to humans. The lionfish is about 15 inches long and lives along rocks and reefs in warm regions.

i'll huff and i'll puff...

Puffer fish are covered with spines. When they are cornered or threatened, they can inflate to twice their normal size.

Porcupine Fish

Don't stop

Many fish can pump water over their gills to get oxygen. Most sharks, however, must swim constantly in order to breathe. By swimming they force water through their mouths and over their gills to get oxygen.

Great White Shark

Smile!

Sharks have several rows of razor-sharp teeth. As a tooth in the front row is worn down, it is replaced by a newer tooth from the back rows.

"A bath may sound swell if you're a shark, bass, or pike.

Blue Shark

No bones about it

Sharks have no bones! Instead, their entire skeleton is made of cartilage, which is the same stiff stuff that makes up the tip of your nose and ears. This makes sharks extremely flexible creatures.

"But taking a bath is not what i like."

Saw Shark

Leopard Shark

21

"**First,** let's get our facts straight," huffed the black-and-white orca, as he twitched his huge tail.

Sperm Whale

Take a deep breath

Whales breathe air through a blowhole at the top of their heads. A blue whale can dive as deep as 1,500 feet and can stay under water for hours at a time.

Think about this

Whales, dolphins, and porpoises are considered some of the smartest creatures in the ocean. The sperm whale has a brain weighing close to 20 pounds—the largest brain of any animal.

Do all whales have teeth?

No! While all dolphins and porpoises have teeth, only some whales have them. There are two types of whales: toothed whales and baleen whales. Baleen is a hard, bonelike substance that acts as a giant filter. Baleen whales filter entire schools of fish, squid, and crustaceans (see page 30). Dolphins, porpoises, and toothed whales catch and eat their food one item at a time.

"I am hardly a fish, but rather a whale!"

Right Whale

Whales, dolphins, and porpoises are not fish! See page 24 to find out why.

Krill

What's for dinner?

The main course for many baleen whales is a small, shrimplike creature called krill. Krill swim in large groups called shoals. Whales simply swim with their mouths open through a shoal of krill. The krill are trapped in the baleen filters. A blue whale may eat up to four tons of krill in a day.

Fish or whale?

The name "whales" also includes dolphins and porpoises. The main difference between fish and whales is that whales are mammals and fish are not, which means that whales, dolphins, and porpoises breathe air like you and me. (Do you remember how fish breathe?) Whales, dolphins, and porpoises are warm-blooded. (Fish are cold-blooded.) Whales, dolphins, and porpoises give birth to live young. (Fish lay eggs.)

Humpback Whales

Rock-a-bye baby...

Newborn baby whales can weigh up to 4,000 pounds and can be 20 feet long. Every day they need to drink over 25 gallons of their mother's milk to get a proper meal.

Extinction?

Whales have been hunted by man since the late 1800s. They were killed for their meat, blubber, and bone. Man hunted whales almost into extinction. In 1987 commercial whaling was outlawed, and today the whales are making a slow comeback. Some nations, however, still hunt whales illegally.

Dall's Porpoise

Go south, young whale

Gray whales make one of the longest migrations of any animal on Earth. They journey 6,000 miles every year from their summer feeding grounds in the Arctic to their winter breeding waters in southern California. Some 20,000 whales make the trip, which takes six to eight weeks. Whales travel in groups called pods.

The big and small of it

The largest animal on Earth is the blue whale. It can grow to be 100 feet long and weigh as much as 190,000 pounds. The harbor porpoise, on the other hand, can be as small as four feet long and 100 pounds.

"You may be a whale," smirked Billy, "but you're a whale who can't hear. Could it be there's some seaweed stuck in your ear?"

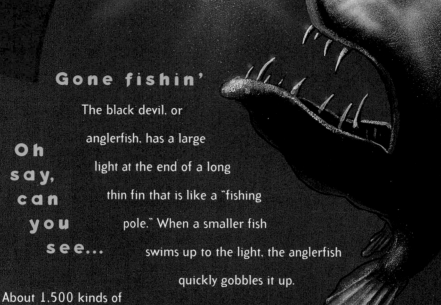

Gone fishin'

The black devil, or anglerfish, has a large light at the end of a long thin fin that is like a "fishing pole." When a smaller fish swims up to the light, the anglerfish quickly gobbles it up.

Oh say, can you see...

About 1,500 kinds of deep-sea fish can produce their own light. These fish have light organs (photophores) that provide glowing light. The lights are made up of billions of glowing bacteria and help the fish to attract prey and find mates.

Anglerfish

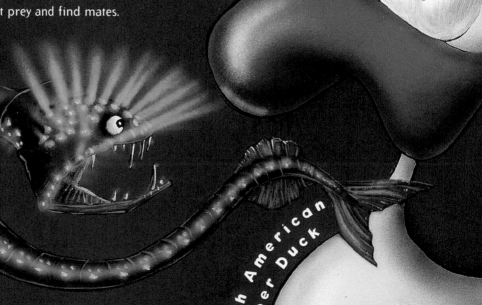

Dragonfish

North American Rubber Duck

"I'll tell you right now, Mr. Whale, for the very last time, i really enjoy the dirt, dust, and grime."

Hatchetfish have eyes that point upward and act like binoculars. They help the hatchetfish scan the water above for small fish. The hatchetfish itself is flat and skinny so it doesn't attract predators from deeper down.

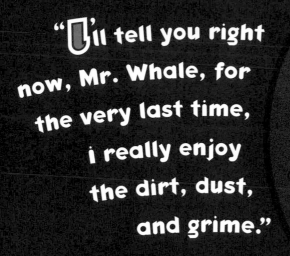

Hatchetfish

Pacific Viperfish

Lunch

Catching prey in the ocean depths is very difficult. Since it may be weeks between meals. some deep-sea fish have stomachs that stretch so they can eat as much as possible when a meal is caught.

Horsing around

The sea horse is a bad swimmer that relies on its ability to change colors to hide from predators and sneak up on prey. Their eyes can move separately, so they can look in two different directions at the same time.

Mr. Mom

During breeding season, the female sea horse lays up to 200 eggs. The male sea horse stores the eggs in his stomach pouch. The baby sea horses are born from two to five weeks later.

Sea Horses

The whale just whispered, "Stop being a stubborn boy, and i'll show you the ways to make bathtime a joy.

"**J**ust listen real close—make a list if you wish—of these great bathtime secrets shared by the fish!"

Manta rays take flight under the water, gracefully beating their fins like a bird beats its wings. Manta rays can grow to a width of over 18 feet and a weight of 3,000 pounds.

Jelly Fish

Manta Rays

Moray eels spend most of their time under ledges or in holes along the coral. Their mouths are full of pointed teeth, yet they generally bite only when bothered.

Moray Eel

sea urchin

"First: Don't be alone when you sit in the tub. Round up some friends who will help you to scrub.

Trash man

Crabs are scavengers and will eat almost anything on the ocean floor.

Crabs, lobsters, and prawns are all crustaceans. They have antennae, jointed legs, and a hard shell protecting their soft inner bodies. The smallest crustaceans are microscopic critters, and the largest are giant spider crabs, which can measure 12 feet across.

Purple Shore Crab

Red Crab

Horseshoe Crab

Oregon Cancer Crab

Come out of your shell

Like children who outgrow their clothes, crustaceans outgrow their shells. Every year they shed (molt) shells that are too small. Crustaceans can also shed a leg or claw that is trapped or injured. The limb will slowly grow back in stages every time the crustacean molts.

"Molly, your boat, Bob, and your rubber duck, Bob, and your rubber duck are very good choices to help do the job."

Molly Dog

California Fiddler Crab

Australian Lobster

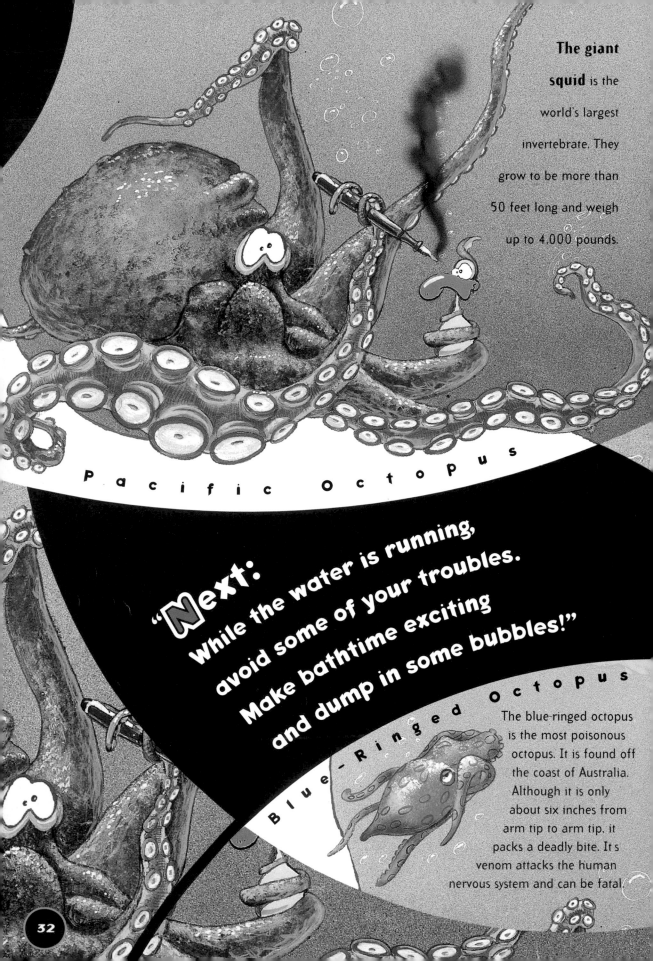

The giant squid is the world's largest invertebrate. They grow to be more than 50 feet long and weigh up to 4,000 pounds.

Pacific Octopus

"Next: while the water is running, avoid some of your troubles. Make bathtime exciting and dump in some bubbles!"

Blue-Ringed Octopus

The blue-ringed octopus is the most poisonous octopus. It is found off the coast of Australia. Although it is only about six inches from arm tip to arm tip, it packs a deadly bite. It s venom attacks the human nervous system and can be fatal.

Which way did he go?

When a squid, octopus, or cuttlefish is being chased by a predator, it squirts a big cloud of dark ink. The cloud confuses the predator so the mollusk can escape. Another strange trait the octopus has is the ability to blend into backgrounds by rapidly changing color and patterns.

If an octopus is red colored that means it is agitated.

Mommy dearest

The female octopus lays eggs only once in her life. When she is three years old, she lays about 50,000 tiny eggs, usually hanging them on the ceiling of a small, underwater cave. She then spends the next six months spraying clean water on the eggs with nozzlelike spouts located on the side of her head. Soon after the babies hatch, the mother dies.

Squid are the fastest mollusk, reaching speeds of 20 miles per hour.

Arm in arm in arm in arm in arm

There are over 150 species of octopus inhabiting Earth's oceans. They use the suckers on their eight arms (tentacles) and their rock-hard beak to hunt and capture crabs and fish. The largest octopus ever found had tentacles spanning over 23 feet in length and weighed over 118 pounds.

"A mountain of bubbles may seem kind of weird, but when wiped on your chin it makes a great bubble beard."

Moon

Gravity

Low tide

High tide

Earth

High tide

Low tide

What causes tides?

If you have been to the ocean, you may have noticed that throughout the day the water level rises (high tide) and then falls (low tide). High tides are caused when the moon's gravity pulls the water away from Earth's surface.

Tug-of-war

There are two high tides happening at the same time on Earth. The side closest to the moon has a high tide, but so does the side farthest from the moon. Just as the moon pulls the water away from Earth on the close side, it also pulls the Earth away from the water on the far side.

All wet

The ocean is a huge body of salt water that covers three-quarters of the Earth.

Gravity

is an invisible force that pulls two objects toward each other. Gravitational pull is determined by how big the two objects are and the distance between them.

How high is the tide?

At certain times during the month the moon and the sun line up in such a way that their gravitational pulls are both pulling in the same direction. When this happens, the stronger gravitational pull causes unusually high tides, or "spring tides." (Spring tides don't necessarily happen in the spring.) When the moon and sun are not pulling in the same direction, their gravitational pulls are working against each other, so the high tides are lower than usual. These tides are called "neap tides."

Mussels

On the right foot

Sea stars and sea urchins have hundreds of tiny tube feet, while limpets and sea snails have a single suction foot.

Scallops

Protected by sharp spines, sea urchins use hundreds of feet to anchor and drag themselves along the rocks. They scavenge for food and graze on seaweeds.

Sand Dollar

Sea urchins

Goby

Limpets

"You see," said the whale, "the secret for fish, beast, and child...

Hermit crabs live in other mollusks' discarded shells. When a hermit crab grows too big for one shell, it looks for a larger shell to move into.

"Us to make bathtime an adventure— let your imagination go wild!"

Sea Anemones

Hermit Crab

Sea Urchins

Prawn

Mountain Crab

Sea Stars

Sea stars (also called starfish) can grow a new arm if one is cut off. This is known as regeneration. Sometimes, even if a sea star is cut in half, the entire missing half will regenerate.

Seal you later

The California sea lion is one of the fastest pinnipeds, traveling at over 20 miles per hour.

Southern Elephant Seal

Southern elephant seals

are the largest species in the pinniped family. Adult males can weigh up to 6,000 pounds. These huge creatures live in the icy Antarctic waters and can be recognized by their large noses. They communicate by using a series of gargles, burps, and whines.

Sea Otter

Sea otters spend much of their time relaxing in kelp beds. Sometimes otters actually wrap themselves in kelp so they won't float away while napping. Otters use rocks to break open the shells of sea urchins, crabs, and other prey.

Pinnipeds

There are over 30 species of pinnipeds inhabiting every ocean in the world. They include seals, sea lions, and walruses. They are comfortable both on land and in the water and have a thick layer of blubber to protect them from freezing water. They are great swimmers and divers and can dive up to half a mile. Even though pinnipeds breathe air, they can stay underwater for 20 to 30 minutes.

A walrus has about 700 hairs on its nose. The hairs are about 35 times thicker than human hair and are used to search for shellfish.

Walrus

Harbor Seal

Billy sat up and yelled, "I see what you mean! I could be the captain of a green submarine, on a top-secret mission to get my toes clean!"

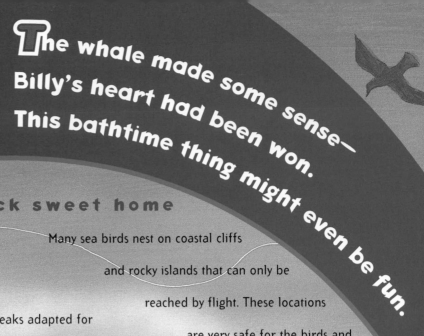

The whale made some sense—
Billy's heart had been won.
This bathtime thing might even be fun.

Rock sweet home

Many sea birds nest on coastal cliffs and rocky islands that can only be reached by flight. These locations are very safe for the birds and also keep them close to the shore where they can hunt for food.

Great white pelicans have beaks adapted for hunting fish. The bottom of the beak is a large pouch. When the pelican dips its bill in the water, the pouch fills with water and small fish. As the bird lifts its head, the pouch squeezes the water out and traps the fish.

Great White Pelican

Whimbrel (sandpiper family)

Common Puffin

Put it on my bill

Ocean birds have bills (beaks) that are made just
for catching and hanging on to fish. Some beaks
have curved tips that keep the fish from
slipping out the end. Others are designed
to hammer open shells, and still others
work like spears. Some birds dive
from as high as 100 feet to spear
and catch small fish.

Albatross

**Billy hugged his Great Dane and gave a loud cheer,
"I think that I'll bathe more than three times a year!"**

Emperor
Penguin

Red-throated Loon

Galápagos Penguin

ANTARCTICA

MAP

**Emperor
penguins**
nest in Antarctica,
where
temperatures
go down to -70
degrees. The female
lays a single egg, and
it is then up to the
male to take care of it. He will balance the egg on top of his feet to keep
it from getting too cold. Sometimes he won't eat or move for nine weeks
until the egg hatches and the female returns to take care of the chick.

The little white tub started for home, leaving behind the soft ocean foam.

Billy shook the whale's fin and said with a grin,

44

The bathroom door opened to reveal Billy's mother. She gave him a glare and then gave him another.

"You've been awfully quiet, young man. Are you causing a scene?" Billy giggled, "No, dearest mother, i'm just getting clean."

She smiled a small smile and disappeared down the hall—not noticing the sea star stuck on the wall.

The end.

About the Authors

Douglas Kelly is a very nice man. He has a fuzzy beard and isn't very tall. (He reminds Ray of a hamster.) Doug spent five years as a set designer for Will Vinton Studios in Portland, Oregon. He learned how to be an artist by watching his father (who is also an artist) and studying real hard at Mount Hood Community College near Portland and Art Center College of Design in Pasadena, California. Doug would like to thank the Academy, his agent, and all the little people that he stepped on to win this award. (When informed that he actually hasn't won anything and that this is an informational paragraph about his personal life, Doug seemed very disappointed.) Doug enjoys golfing, saving cats from the tops of very tall trees, spending time with Victoria, and creating world peace.

Ray Nelson is a very big person (six-feet-four-inches tall) and has always loved to draw strange characters and write silly stories. He drew on homework. He drew on walls. And he drew on his little brother, Troy. Ray spent five years as an animator and designer for Will Vinton Studios in Portland, Oregon, before starting his own business, Flying Rhinoceros, Inc. Besides writing and illustrating, Ray also speaks to thousands of schoolchildren about cartooning, writing, and the importance of persistence, self-esteem, and confidence. Today Ray spends most of his time entertaining his daughter, Alexandria, entertaining his wife, Theresa, and just trying to stay out of trouble. Occasionally he might be found cleaning up the hair and drool that has been scattered about his house by Molly the Great Dane.

Ben Adams

Acknowledgments

A special thank you to our very good friends, Gene Kelly, Ray and Chris Nelson Sr., and Edna Nelson; Theresa Nelson, harbormaster; Victoria Collins, crustacean wrangler; Mike and Holly McLane, explosives experts; Kevin Atkinson, Billy's stunt double; Ben Adams, assistant to Molly Dog; Susan Ring, tuna tuner; Jacelen Pete, stunt double for Bob the rubber duck; Shaunna Griggs, rubber-duck trainer; Mark Hansen, fish wrangler; Troy Nelson, pinniped choreographer; and Kelly Kuntz and all the wonderful kids at Hiteon Elementary School in Beaverton, Oregon. This project would never have set sail if it weren't for the contributions of these wonderful individuals. Thank you! And a very special thank you to Alexandria Nelson for the drool, diapers, and a whole new perspective on children.

About Flying Rhinoceros Books

Flying Rhinoceros books are dedicated to the education and entertainment of elementary school students. Flying Rhinoceros also offers curriculum/activity packs to accompany all the books.

For more information or to request a catalog, please contact Beyond Words Publishing, Inc.

Beyond Words Publishing, inc.
4443 NE Airport Road
Hillsboro, Oregon 97124-6074
503-693-8700 / 1-800-284-9673

Other books from Flying Rhinoceros:
Connie & Bonnie's Birthday Blastoff (Outer space)
Greetings from America: Postcards from Donovan Willoughby (U.S. geography)
Wooden Teeth and Jelly Beans: The Tupperman Files (U.S. presidents)
Shrews Can't Hoop!? (Self-esteem)
A Dinosaur Ate My Homework (Dinosaurs)
Cartoon Handbook and Field Guide (How to cartoon)